Robot

–Friend or Foe?

Sarah Fleming

OXFORD
UNIVERSITY PRESS

OXFORD
UNIVERSITY PRESS

Great Clarendon Street, Oxford OX2 6DP

Oxford University Press is a department of the University of Oxford.
It furthers the University's objective of excellence in research, scholarship,
and education by publishing worldwide in

Oxford   New York

Auckland   Cape Town   Dar es Salaam   Hong Kong   Karachi
Kuala Lumpur   Madrid   Melbourne   Mexico City   Nairobi
New Delhi   Shanghai   Taipei   Toronto

With offices in

Argentina   Austria   Brazil   Chile   Czech Republic   France   Greece
Guatemala   Hungary   Italy   Japan   Poland   Portugal   Singapore
South Korea   Switzerland   Thailand   Turkey   Ukraine   Vietnam

Oxford is a registered trade mark of Oxford University Press
in the UK and in certain other countries

British Library Cataloguing in Publication Data

Data available

ISBN 978-0-19-917937-4

9 10 8

Printed in China by Imago

Paper used in the production of this book is a natural,
recyclable product made from wood grown in sustainable forests.
The manufacturing process conforms to the environmental
regulations of the country or origin.

Acknowledgements

The publisher would like to thank the following for permission to reproduce
photographs: **p1** Photodisc/OUP, **p3** Corbis/Hulton Deutsch Collection, **p4** Corbis/Frank Trapper, **p5** Corbis/Ariel
Skelly, **p6** © 2005 Marvel/Corbis, **p7** Getty/Getty Images Entertainment, **p8** Corbis/Zuma, **p9**t Corbis/Jim Sugar, b
Science Photo Library, **p11** Corbis RF, **p12** Corbis/Reuters, **p13**l Getty Images, c Getty Imagbes/AFP, r
Corbis/Reuters, **p14** Corbis/Owen Franken, **p15** Corbis/Reuters, **p16** Corbis/Reuters, **p17** NASA, **p18**t Getty
Images/National Geographic, b Corbis/Reuters, **p19**t Corbis/Roger Ressmeyer, b Redzone, **p20**t Corbis/Yiogos
Ksahalis/Reuters, b Getty Images/AFP, **p21** Corbis/Bureau L.A. Collection, **p22**l Corbis/Louie Psihoyos, cl
Corbis/Lindsay Hebberd, cr Corbis/Reuters, r Corbis/Miyoko Oyashiki, **p24** Corbis/Vo Trung Dung, **p25**l Getty
Images, c Corbis/Digital Art, r Getty Images, **p26**t Getty Images, c Corbis/Lowell Georgia, r Corbis/Digital Art, **p27**
Corbis/Reuters, **p28**t Corbis/Wyman Ira, b Corbis/Gordon David, **p29**t Roger Quinn & Matthew Birch, Biorobotics
Lab. Cast Western Reserve University, b Cardiff University, **p30** Valiant Technology, **p30/31** Getty Images

Cover photography by: Corbis/Digital Art

Illustrations by: **p4**, **p5**, **p10** Barking Dog Art, **p6** Bill Greenhead, **p8**, **p15** Paul Ogilby/Apple Agency

Design by John Walker

Every effort has been made to contact copyright holders of material reproduced in this book. If notified,
the publishers will be pleased to rectify any errors or omissions at the earliest opportunity

Contents

Introduction

Robots are machines that can be programmed to do certain jobs.

'Pilot'

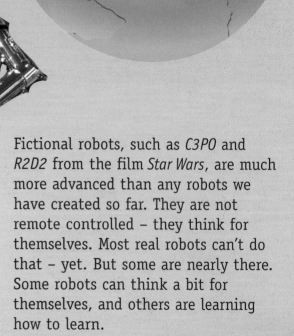

Satellite

We live in an age when a pilot can fly a robot plane that is half-way across the world and make it bomb a specific target.

Fictional robots, such as *C3PO* and *R2D2* from the film *Star Wars*, are much more advanced than any robots we have created so far. They are not remote controlled – they think for themselves. Most real robots can't do that – yet. But some are nearly there. Some robots can think a bit for themselves, and others are learning how to learn.

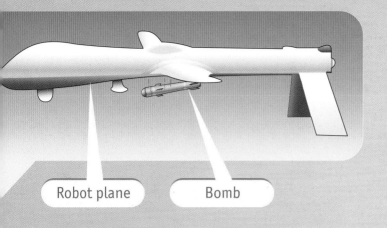

Robot plane

Bomb

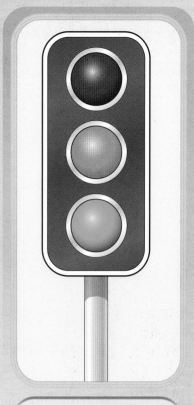

The 'hole in the wall' money machine and the computer printer are probably the most used robots in the world. They may not look like your idea of a robot, but they *are* very basic robots - they are machines built to do certain things (give you money/print a page) with computer brains which tell them when and what to do (how much money/what to print).

Traffic robots

In South Africa, traffic lights are called 'robots'!

This book looks at where and when we use robots and how advanced they are becoming.

20th century view of robots

The idea of making robots to work for us took off with scientific advances made in the 20th century. By the middle of that century some people thought that robots would be doing many everyday tasks for us by AD 2000.

Others thought that robots would learn how to think for themselves. Science fiction writers wondered what would happen if robots tried to take over the world – or the universe!

In this 1965 cartoon, robots are fighting people for control of the world.

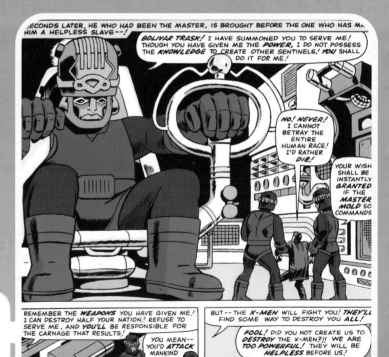

SECONDS LATER, HE WHO HAD BEEN THE MASTER, IS BROUGHT BEFORE THE ONE WHO HAS M... HIM A HELPLESS SLAVE--!

BOLIVAR TRASK! I HAVE SUMMONED YOU TO SERVE ME! THOUGH YOU HAVE GIVEN ME THE POWER, I DO NOT POSSESS THE KNOWLEDGE TO CREATE OTHER SENTINELS! YOU SHALL DO IT FOR ME!

NO! NEVER! I CANNOT BETRAY THE ENTIRE HUMAN RACE! I'D RATHER DIE!

YOUR WISH SHALL BE INSTANTLY GRANTED IF THE MASTER MOLD SO COMMANDS

REMEMBER THE WEAPONS YOU HAVE GIVEN ME! I CAN DESTROY HALF YOUR NATION! REFUSE TO SERVE ME, AND YOU'LL BE RESPONSIBLE FOR THE CARNAGE THAT RESULTS!

YOU MEAN-- YOU'D ATTACK MANKIND ??!

BUT-- THE X-MEN WILL FIGHT YOU! THEY'LL FIND SOME WAY TO DESTROY YOU ALL!

FOOL! DID YOU NOT CREATE US TO DESTROY THE X-MEN?!! WE ARE TOO POWERFUL! THEY WILL BE HELPLESS BEFORE US!

What do you think?

The Three Laws of Robotics were written by science fiction writer Isaac Asimov in the 1940s:

1) A robot may not harm a human being, or, by doing nothing, let a human being come to harm

2) A robot must obey the orders given to it by human beings, except where an order would be against the First Law

3) A robot must protect itself, as long as this is not against the First or Second Law.

We don't need these rules yet, because robots don't think for themselves.

If robots get clever, do you think they should be made to work to these rules?

Throughout this book you'll find boxes like this with questions about robots' rights for you to think about.

Will Smith starred in a film version of Isaac Asimov's book, *I, Robot*.

Factory robots

Robots are very useful for factory work because they:

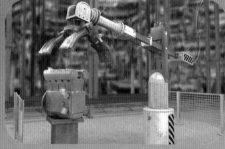

can lift heavy things like engines without hurting their backs

don't mind doing the same boring thing again and again... and again...

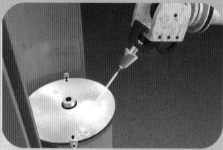

can work very precisely

can spray paint, weld things and do other 'dangerous' tasks with no health or safety risks.

Probably the best known robots in the world today make cars.

Making cars

Ten years ago ninety per cent of all robots made cars. Today, only fifty per cent of robots are used in the car industry.

A robot 'taxi' delivers more paper to a newspaper printing press while the human worker does the crossword.

Airbus assembly factory, Toulouse, France.

Robota

The word robot comes from a Czech word, *robota*, which means 'forced work'. It was first used in a 1920s play which looked at whether machines should take over people's work or not. People are still discussing this problem today.

A journalist who visited this aircraft assembly factory said:

"I went into this huge aircraft hanger and...it was silent! I'd expected noise and bustle. Instead, huge robots were quietly attaching the wings to a plane, precisely, to a fraction of a millimetre. In one corner, a man sat in front of a computer – he was the only person in there."

What do you think?

How would you feel if your work was given to a robot and you had no new work to go to?

What does a simple robot need?

A robot needs:

A Power to move the parts. Robots are usually powered by electricity. Parts are moved by air or water pressure

B A computer brain, or 'controller', to tell it what to do

C One or more moveable parts, e.g. an arm

D A tool, usually at the end of the arm. The tool can be a hand, a blowtorch, a screwdriver – almost anything. Some robots have changeable tools. Some have many tools on more than one arm

E Sensors, to tell the controller where the tool is and what it is doing. Sensors can be for touch, sight (e.g. cameras), sound, smell – even taste. They can also detect **radioactivity** or movement.

Degrees of Freedom

Robots must be able to move one or more parts of themselves. One degree of freedom allows you to move up and down, or left and right. A robot arm usually has six degrees of freedom.

This robot has degrees of freedom that let the:

1. whole 'arm' rotate
2. main 'arm' go up and down
3. 'elbow' bend
4. 'wrist' go left and right
5. 'wrist' go up and down
6. 'wrist' rotate.

How many degrees of freedom does a human arm have?
(Answer on page 32)

Movement

Six degrees of movement is fine for a robot that is welding parts of a car. But what about robots that need to move about? Robots need to be stable and not fall over when they move.

Many robots today have wheels. This usually means they can only move on flat surfaces. Some have 'smart' wheels which let the robot tilt to get over small bumps. But wheels can't climb over anything higher than half their own height.

Robot *Asimo* has 26 degrees of freedom which lets it do complex things like use stairs.

The most common ways of moving about are:-

Method		
Wheels	Tracks	Legs
Advantages		
• Easy to make • Can support a lot of weight	• Good on uneven ground	• Good on uneven ground • Able to climb stairs • Easier to navigate than tracks • The more legs, the more stable the robot
Disadvantages		
• Not good on uneven ground	• Heavy, bulky	• Heavy, need more motors • More difficult to balance and program
Cost		
• Cheap	• Expensive	• Expensive
Example		
Build your own roving robot with wheels	Japan's largest rescue robot moves on tracks	This four-legged robot may be sent to Mars

Complex movement

Looking for survivors is dangerous – the building might collapse even more at any second.

Earthquake disasters

Think how useful it would be to get a robot into the small spaces in collapsed buildings. A robot could test for signs of life below piles of rubble and even monitor the rubble to see how safe it is, before people started to work at removing it.

But what's the best shape for such a robot? How should it move?

The newest designs for rescue robots include ones which are made out of 'mini-robot' **modules** which can adapt to where they are by re-arranging themselves. Scientists hope the robots may even be able to form protective shells around victims while they wait to be rescued.

This robot can change the way its modules join together, depending on the surface it is crossing. It becomes:

1. a snake for worming up and through a hole in rubble

3. a cartwheel on flat ground to travel quickly

2. separate smaller snakes, to search different areas

4. a spider for climbing over piles of rubble.

When the robot is in snake formation it can move in different snakey ways – it can undulate, like a normal snake, or move like a sidewinder.

Modular robots might be perfect for doing research on the surfaces of planets. They could cross the ground easily and even tunnel into the planet to take samples.

A model of NASA's module research robot. Could this be the next robot on Mars?

Mars exploration

Two identical robots landed on Mars in January 2004. This is an artist's impression of one of the robots on Mars' surface.

Robots have made several trips to Mars. They have travelled around, taken samples and photographs, mapped the land and searched for signs of water and life. As well as developing robots like those on pages 13 and 15 for future missions, scientists are developing huge inflatable ball-type robots that could be blown about the surface of Mars by the wind.

Smart wheels

The most recent Mars robots had six 'smart' wheels which let them tilt up to 45° on uneven surfaces without falling over.

Space exploration

Robots have explored the solar system far further than manned spacecraft have gone. For example, the *Cassini* robot, launched in 1997, reached Saturn in 2004. It is still sending back information.

Robots are also used by astronauts. As well as robotic arms helping in experiments and repairs, there are rescue robots. They're even developing a 'robonaut'!

What do you think?

Robonauts, not Astronauts?

Some people say that in the future we should send *only* robots into space. The International Space Station cost over $100 billion. Sending robots is much cheaper than sending people; robots are less likely to damage **ecosystems** on other planets because they don't have any **biological matter** which might interfere with possible life there; astronauts have died in accidents in space.

BUT: Can astronauts do more than robots can? Could they discover things that robots couldn't? What would the world be like today if humans had never bothered to explore it?

Difficult and dangerous

Robots are especially useful in difficult and dangerous situations.

They can be built to:
- cope with radioactivity
- be very strong
- cope with very hot or very cold places.

And they:
- don't breathe air, so can be exposed to smoke and poisonous gas
- might break, but they can't die.

Difficult situations
Robots help scientists to explore the frozen Arctic, Antarctica and the depths of the oceans.

Dangerous situations
Robots help to clear mine fields.

The operator stands behind thick lead glass and lets the robot arms pack this radioactive material.

The worst radioactive disaster of all time was when, in 1986, a nuclear reactor at the power station at Chernobyl, Ukraine, exploded. Twenty years later the station is still highly radioactive. More than 100,000 people had to leave their homes and many have not been able to go back home yet. Land as far away as Wales, UK, was contaminated with radioactivity.

For many years people were sent into the remains of the station to test the levels of radioactivity, but the levels were still so high that this was very dangerous, even in special suits. Since 1999, robot *Pioneer* has been making trips into the remains instead. Robots may help to clear up the station in the future.

Security and soldiers

Remote-controlled robots check out car bombs and suspicious packages in countries worldwide. The robot can detonate any bomb while the operator stays a safe distance away.

Robot guards are fitted with movement detectors. They don't fall asleep on night duty and don't mind rain or cold weather.

Japanese guard dog *Banryu* (meaning 'guard dragon') has fifty sensors (including smell sensors) to detect burglars and can send alarms to its master's mobile phone!

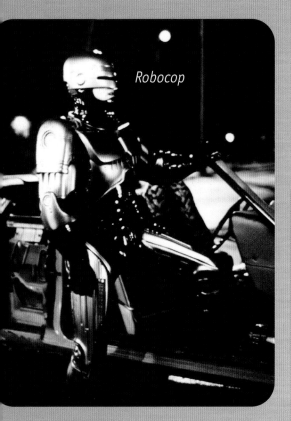

Robocop

What do you think?

Most countries have armies, but should they have robot soldiers?
Do you think it would be easier to start a war if you could fight with robots instead of people? Is this a good thing?

We don't have robot policemen yet, but there are robot soldiers...

Robot soldiers patrol Gulf

7 April 2005

Robots carrying machine guns have been sent to patrol danger zones in Iraq. The United States army has sent 18 *Swords* (Special Weapons Observation Reconnaissance Detection Systems) to help its forces combat terrorism.

Swords are one metre tall and equipped with M249 or M240 rifles. They have four cameras, with night-vision and zoom lenses. They can travel over rough ground and barbed wire.

Robots don't eat or sleep. They don't get frightened, and they are more accurate than a soldier.

A human operator out of range of danger operates the *Sword* using remote control.

Swords' batteries last for four hours and each 'soldier' costs US$200,000.

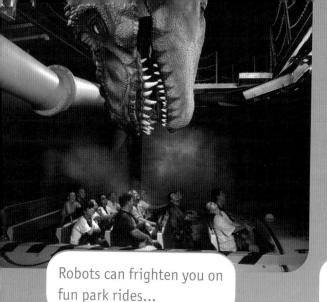

Robots can frighten you on fun park rides...

... tell your fortune on the street...

Entertainment

Robots can come in all shapes and sizes. If you could invent a fun robot, what would it do? Pick some features from those shown here and design your own robot.
Think of other features of your own, too.

Size
- Cat-sized
- Big as a house
- Car-sized
- Pocket-sized
- Fit in your ear

Move-ment
- Climb
- Drive
- Crawl
- Fly
- Swim

What would

...or play with you at home.

How about having a robot fish? Then you wouldn't have to clean the aquarium!

you pick?

Sensors

- Touch
- Sight
- Sound
- Movement
- Taste

It would:

- Record what it sees and hears
- Respond to your voice
- Teach you things
- Learn how to play your favourite games
- Copy your movements

You could:

- Play with it
- Cuddle it
- Make it do your homework
- Spy with it!
- Race it

Health and medicine

Robots now help surgeons operate, monitor patients, help with the rounds and soon may be found in a person near you!

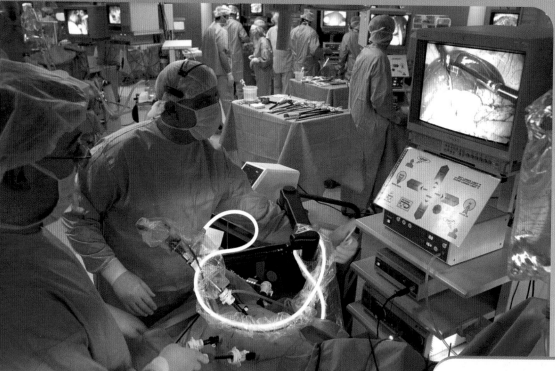

Advantages of robots in surgery. They:
- can be very small and get into the body without cutting too much muscle. This makes it easier for the patient to recover from surgery
- are very accurate, judging distances more finely than the human hand
- don't get tired and start to wobble like human hands might
- can be more thoroughly **sterilised** than human hands.

Surgeons look at a screen to see inside the patient's body. A robot performs the operation, instructed by the surgeon's voice.

This robot doctor has a camera and a TV screen for a head. The two-way video lets the doctor see and talk to the patient and vice versa.

This robot 'suit' helps people walk. Sensors read the electrical signals sent by the brain to the muscles. They help the muscles to move – even before the muscles themselves react!

In the future, tiny robots (**nanobots**) may be injected into your body to repair it from the inside.

What do you think?
Blurring humans and robots

We've now reached a stage where scientists can add wires to a rat's brain and make a rat directly control a robot. In the future, could we all have **implants** and be trained to control a robot directly by just thinking about it? The implants might work the other way round too – perhaps we could have information directly inserted into our brains without having to learn anything! Is this a good idea?

Anywhere – everywhere?

Robots seem to be reaching all aspects of human life. You can find them in fields and factories, homes and hospitals. They're in the sky, underground, in the sea and on the streets. They do everything from shearing sheep to acting as air hostesses. And they're getting more and more helpful.

Planting rice

Serving pizza

On a smaller scale this robot 'spy fly' can reach places other robots cannot go...

Life of a woolly jumper

Robots can shear the sheep, spin and dye the wool and roll it into balls. Robots can help design the jumper, knit the jumper and pack it up to send to a shop. They can track the jumper from the factory to the shop. Robots can stack the jumper on the shop shelf, and the till (a basic robot) can tell the assistant what the jumper costs and what change to give. In fact robots can do everything except drive the lorry from the factory to the shop and sell the jumper. (Oh – and they probably wouldn't wear it!)

This owl-shaped receptionist can remember guests' faces and names and talk about topics it researches on the Internet, such as the weather.

What do you think?

Will there be more exciting, rewarding jobs for the people who lose their current jobs to robots? Or will they be unemployed?

The future?

Most of today's robots CAN'T:
- think for themselves
- make complicated decisions
- learn from mistakes
- get their own power
- adapt to where they are.

Scientists are trying to get robots to do these things. And some of today's most advanced robots can do some of these things.

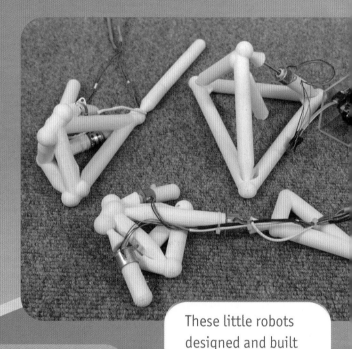

These little robots designed and built themselves!

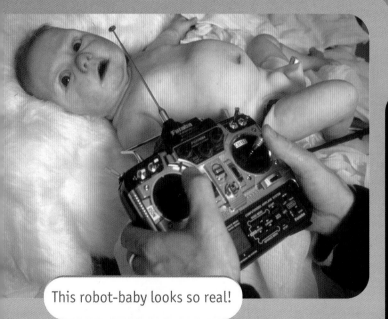

This robot-baby looks so real!

What do you think?

Should robots get more lifelike, or should we be able to tell the difference between a person and a machine?

Robots that eat?

Most robots are powered by electricity. But what about robots that eat plant or animal matter as their power source – like us?

A robot called *Slugbot* is designed to catch slugs. When it has caught one, it scrapes it into a container. Back at its base, the slugs **decompose** into a natural gas which is turned into electricity to power *Slugbot's* next hunting expedition!

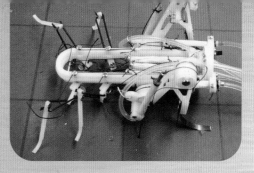

Biobots

Scientists have developed a robot cricket that not only looks and acts like a cricket – it thinks like one too. The cells of the cricket's brain have been copied to learn how it thinks.

Lucy was made out of five home computers. She has 50,000 'brain cells' and one 'working' eye. Her inventor is teaching her how to think. After three years of training, *Lucy* can tell the difference between an apple and a banana.

Make a robot

Robot kits

There are plenty of robot-making kits in the shops today. Make-it-at-home robot kits are quite sophisticated. You can create robots that can be operated from a remote control by infrared light, for example, or by your voice.

You've probably already programmed a robot at school, but maybe you called it a turtle.

Robot makers will use almost anything to make a robot, from the engine of an old washing machine to the circuits in an old electronic toy. (Just remember to ask first!)

So, with the help of some wire strippers, pliers, alligator clips and the odd battery, you could make your own robot to do...whatever you can think of!

Glossary

biological matter – substances made from living plants or animals

decompose – to decay or rot

ecosystem – a system of interacting living things in a particular habitat

implant – something put inside a living thing

module – a unit, a section

nanobot – a very tiny robot

NASA – the National Aeronautics and Space Administration of the United States of America

radioactivity – the state of being radioactive – sending out energy or particles which can be dangerous to health

robot – a machine built and programmed to perform certain jobs

sterilise – to make free from germs

There are even events for you to compete in with your home-made robot.

Index

Answer to page 11: A human arm has seven degrees of movement.